LEARNING FRENCH FOR SCHOOL STUDENTS

DR DHEERAJ MEHROTRA

Contents

Preface

Multilingualism is more vital than ever in an interconnected world. "Learning FRENCH For School Students" pleasantly and enjoyingly introduces young learners to the lovely French language. This book gives schoolchildren a good foundation in French vocabulary, grammar, and pronunciation. We aspire to inspire a lifelong love of language study through interactive exercises, colourful visuals, and relatable examples.

This book is tailored to children's learning preferences, making learning French easier while having fun. Since each chapter builds on the preceding one, language comprehension is progressive and complete. We encourage young learners to join us on this adventure of learning.

As you read "Learning FRENCH For School Students," we encourage parents and educators to participate. You may establish a helpful learning atmosphere that fosters curiosity and passion. This book should become a staple in your classroom, inspiring young people to appreciate the French language and culture.

Start learning French!

Author

CHAPTER ONE

THE FRENCH ALPHABET

The French Alphabet

The French alphabet consists of 26 letters, identical to the English alphabet. However, the pronunciation of these letters can differ significantly. Below is a list of the French letters, English equivalents and pronunciation guides.

Letter	French Name	Pronunciation (Approximate)
A	ah	/a/
B	bé	/be/
C	cé	/se/

| D | dé | /de/ |

| E | e | /ə/ (schwa) |

| F | effe | /ef/ |

| G | gé | /ʒe/ |

| H | ache | /a ʃ/ |

| I | i | /i/ |

| J | ji | /ʒi/ |

| K | ka | /ka/ |

| L | elle | /ɛl/ |

| M | emme | /ɛm/ |

| N | enne | /ɛn/ |

| O | o | /o/ |

| P | pé | /pe/ |

| Q | ku | /ky/ |

| R | erre | / ɛ ʁ/ |

| S | esse | / ɛ s/ |

| T | té | /te/ |

| U | u | /y/ |

| V | vé | /ve/ |

| W | double vé | /dublə ve/ |

| X | iks | /iks/ |

| Y | i grec | /i g ʁ ɛ k/ |

| Z | zède | /z ɛ d/ |

Comprendre l'alphabet français

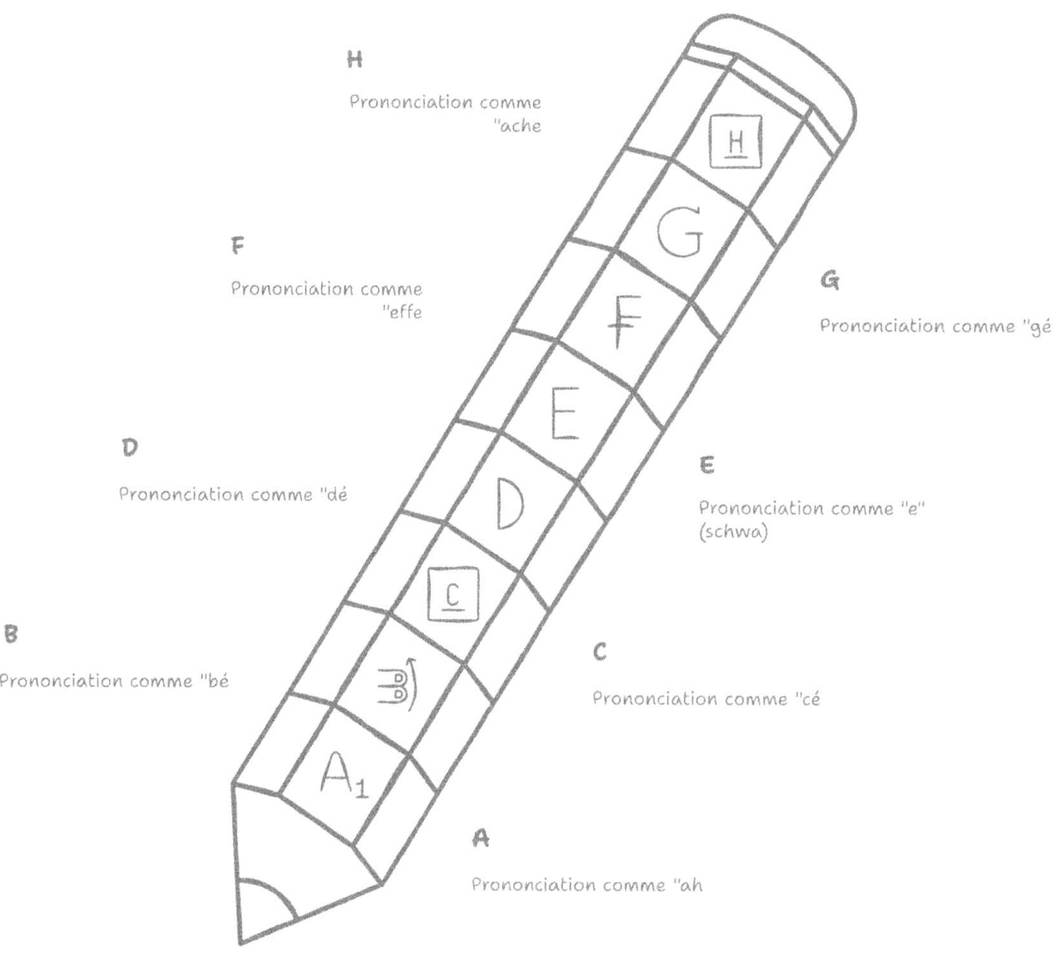

Pronunciation Guide for the French Alphabet

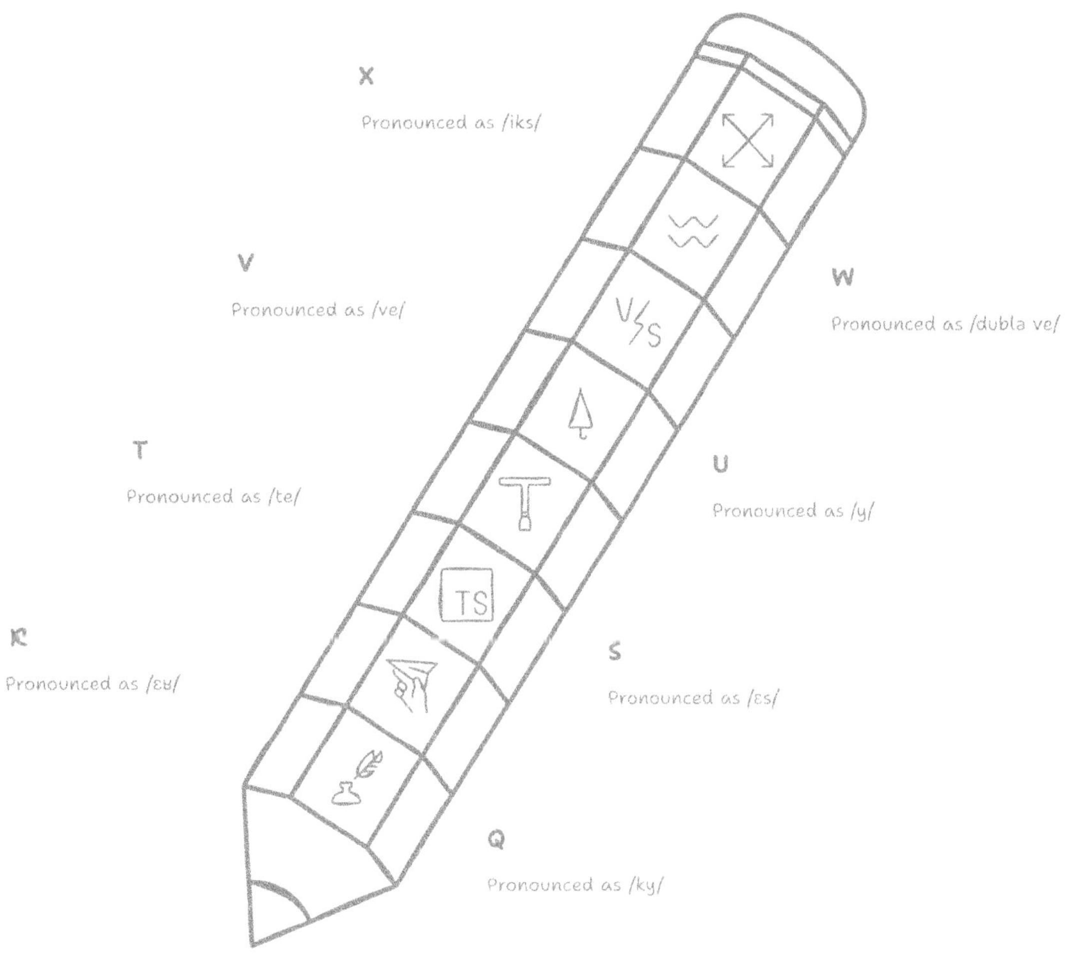

Pronunciation Guide for the French Alphabet

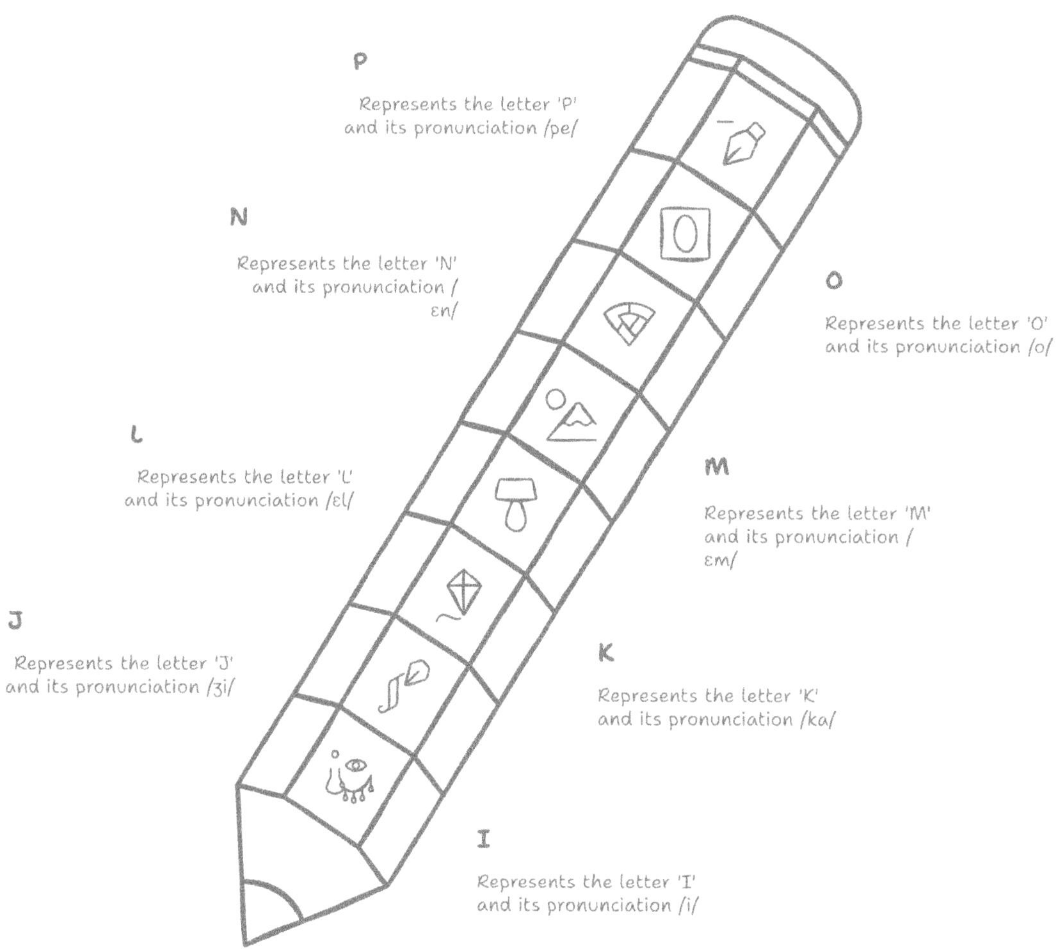

Multiple Choice Questions (MCQs)

1. How many letters are in the French alphabet?
a) 24
b) 25
c) 26
d) 27
Answer: c) 26

2. How is the letter "J" pronounced in French?
a) /ʒe/
b) /ʒi/
c) /ji/
d) /i/
Answer: b) /ʒi/

3. What is the French name for the letter "H"?
a) ache
b) hache
c) hâte
d) hâtech
Answer: a) ache

4. The pronunciation of the letter "E" in French is closest to which sound?
a) /ə/ (schwa)
b) /e/
c) /o/
d) /ɛ/
Answer: a) /ə/

5. How do you say "W" in French?
a) double u
b) double vé
c) deux vé
d) wé
Answer: b) double vé

6. What is the correct pronunciation of "R" in French?
a) /ɛʁ/

b) /ɛr/

c) /ær/

d) /ʀ/

Answer: a) /ɛʁ/

7. What is the French equivalent of the letter "Q"?

a) qui

b) qu

c) ku

d) ky

Answer: c) ku

8. Which letter is pronounced as /iks/ in French?

a) X

b) Z

c) W

d) V

Answer: a) X

9. What is the correct French pronunciation of "C"?

a) /ke/

b) /se/

c) /ce/

d) /ʃe/

Answer: b) /se/

10. How do you pronounce "G" in French?

a) /ge/

b) /ʒe/

c) /ʃe/

d) /ji/

Answer: b) /ʒe/

11. Which of the following is the French pronunciation of "T"?

a) /te/

b) /t/

c) /tə/

d) /ti/

Answer: a) /te/

12. What is the French equivalent of the letter "I"?

a) /i/

b) /y/

c) /e/

d) /ɛ/

Answer: a) /i/

13. What is the correct pronunciation of "O" in French?

a) /ɔ/

b) /o/

c) /u/

d) /ou/

Answer: b) /o/

14. Which of the following letters is pronounced as /ɛs/?

a) S

b) F

c) P

d) N

Answer: a) S

15. Which letter is pronounced as /ve/?

a) W

b) V

c) U

d) T

Answer: b) V

16. What is the French pronunciation of "Y"?

a) /i ɡʁɛk/

b) /i grɛc/

c) /y grek/

d) /i grek/

Answer: d) /i grek/

17. How is the letter "F" pronounced in French?

a) /ef/

b) /ɛf/

c) /fe/

d) /fə/

Answer: a) /ef/

18. What is the pronunciation of "M" in French?

a) /m/

b) /ɛm/

c) /me/

d) /mɛ/

Answer: b) /ɛm/

19. How do you pronounce "L" in French?

a) /l/

b) /ɛl/

c) /le/

d) /lɛ/

Answer: b) /ɛl/

20. What is the French pronunciation of "D"?

a) /d/

b) /de/

c) /di/

d) /də/

Answer: b) /de/

21. Which of the following letters is pronounced as /dublə ve/?

a) X

b) W

c) V

d) U

Answer: b) W

22. What is the correct pronunciation of "Z" in French?

a) /zɛd/

b) /zed/

c) /zid/

d) /zaid/

Answer: a) /zɛd/

23. Which letter is pronounced as /ɛʁ/?

a) S

b) R

c) P

d) M

Answer: b) R

24. The pronunciation /ky/ corresponds to which letter?

a) Q

b) G

c) K

d) L

Answer: a) Q

25. How is the letter "N" pronounced in French?

a) /n/

b) /ɛn/

c) /ne/

d) /nɛ/

Answer: b) /ɛn/

NUMBERS AND COUNTING

Basic Numbers

English Numbers

0 - Zero

1 - One

2 - Two

3 - Three

4 - Four

5 - Five

6 - Six

7 - Seven

8 - Eight

9 - Nine

10 - Ten

French Numbers

0 - Zéro

1 - Un

2 - Deux

3 - Trois

4 - Quatre

5 - Cinq

6 - Six

7 - Sept

8 - Huit

9 - Neuf

10 - Dix

Counting from 11 to 20

<u>*English*</u>

11 - Eleven

12 - Twelve

13 - Thirteen

14 - Fourteen

15 - Fifteen

16 - Sixteen

17 - Seventeen

18 - Eighteen

19 - Nineteen

20 - Twenty

<u>*French*</u>

11 - Onze

12 - Douze

13 - Treize

14 - Quatorze

15 - Quinze

16 - Seize

17 - Dix-sept

18 - Dix-huit

19 - Dix-neuf

20 - Vingt

Tens

English

30 - Thirty

40 - Forty

50 - Fifty

60 - Sixty

70 - *Seventy*

80 - *Eighty*

90 - *Ninety*

100 - *One Hundred*

French

30 - *Trente*

40 - *Quarante*

50 - *Cinquante*

60 - *Soixante*

70 - *Soixante-dix*

80 - *Quatre-vingts*

90 - Quatre-vingt-dix

100 - Cent

Counting Beyond 100

English

101 - One Hundred One

200 - Two Hundred

1,000 - One Thousand

10,000 - Ten Thousand

French

101 - Cent un

200 - Deux cents

1,000 - Mille

10,000 - Dix mille

Multiple Choice Questions (MCQs)

What is the French word for "Seven"?
a) Sept
b) Six
c) Huit
d) Cinq
Answer: a) Sept
What is "Quarante" in English?
a) 30
b) 40
c) 50
d) 60
Answer: b) 40
How do you say "Ten" in French?
a) Onze
b) Dix
c) Douze
d) Cinq
Answer: b) Dix
What is the English equivalent of "Soixante-dix"?
a) 60
b) 70
c) 80
d) 90
Answer: b) 70
What number does "Vingt" represent in English?
a) 10
b) 15

c) 20

d) 25

Answer: c) 20

What is the correct translation of "Eighty" in French?

a) Soixante-dix

b) Quatre-vingts

c) Quarante

d) Cinquante

Answer: b) Quatre-vingts

How do you say "50" in French?

a) Cinquante

b) Soixante

c) Quarante

d) Trente

Answer: a) Cinquante

What does "Onze" mean in English?

a) Eleven

b) Twelve

c) Thirteen

d) Fourteen

Answer: a) Eleven

What is "Dix-sept" in English?

a) 15

b) 16

c) 17

d) 18

Answer: c) 17

Translate "Fourteen" into French.

a) Quatorze

b) Quinze

c) Douze

d) Treize

Answer: a) Quatorze

How do you say "One Hundred" in French?

a) Mille

b) Cent

c) Dix mille

d) Deux cents

Answer: b) Cent

What is "Dix mille" in English?

a) One thousand

b) Ten thousand

c) One hundred thousand

d) One million

Answer: b) Ten thousand

What is the French translation of "Nine"?

a) Huit

b) Neuf

c) Dix

d) Sept

Answer: b) Neuf

How do you say "Thirty" in French?

a) Trente

b) Quarante

c) Cinquante

d) Soixante

Answer: a) Trente

What is "Seize" in English?

a) 14

b) 15

c) 16

d) 17

Answer: c) 16

How do you say "200" in French?

a) Cent un

b) Deux cents

c) Mille

d) Dix mille

Answer: b) Deux cents

What does "Cinq" mean in English?

a) Four

b) Five

c) Six

d) Seven

Answer: b) Five

How do you say "One Thousand" in French?

a) Cent un

b) Mille

c) Deux cents

d) Dix mille

Answer: b) Mille

What is "Quatre" in English?

a) Four

b) Five

c) Six

d) Seven

Answer: a) Four

Translate "Twelve" into French.

a) Onze

b) Douze

c) Treize

d) Quatorze

Answer: b) Douze

How do you say "Ninety" in French?

a) Quatre-vingts

b) Soixante-dix

c) Quatre-vingt-dix

d) Cinquante

Answer: c) Quatre-vingt-dix

What is the French word for "Six"?

a) Sept

b) Huit

c) Six

d) Cinq

Answer: c) Six

How do you say "One" in French?

a) Un

b) Deux

c) Trois

d) Quatre

Answer: a) Un

What is "Treize" in English?

a) Eleven

b) Twelve

c) Thirteen

d) Fourteen

Answer: c) Thirteen

What does "Huit" mean in English?

a) Seven

b) Eight

c) Nine

d) Ten

Answer: b) Eight

CHAPTER THREE

COMMON PHRASES FOR DAILY USE

Polite Expressions in English and French

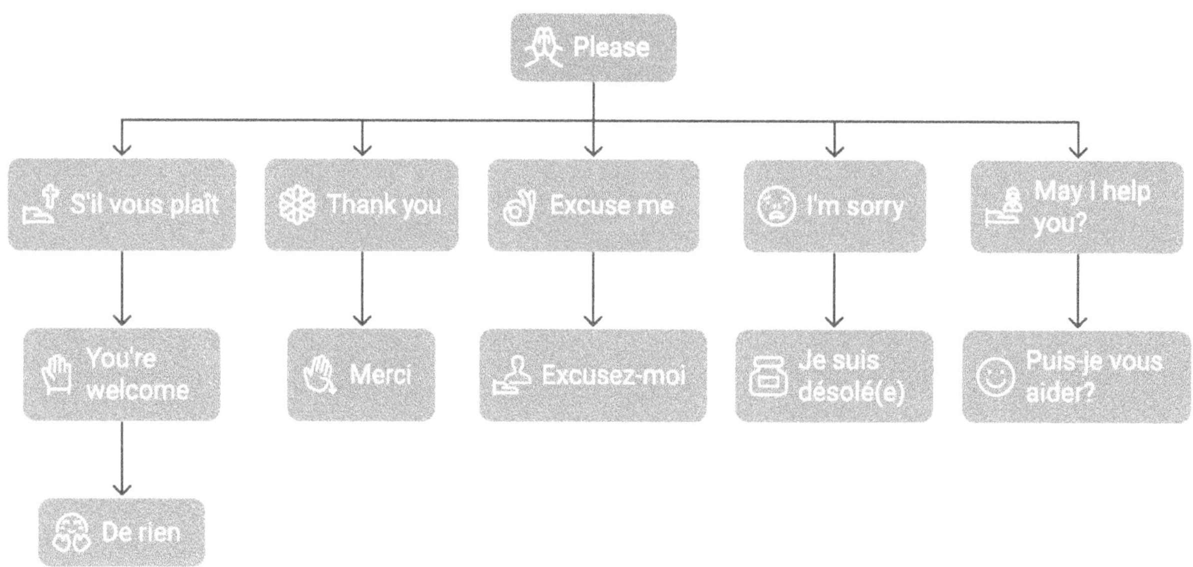

Everyday Interactions in English and French

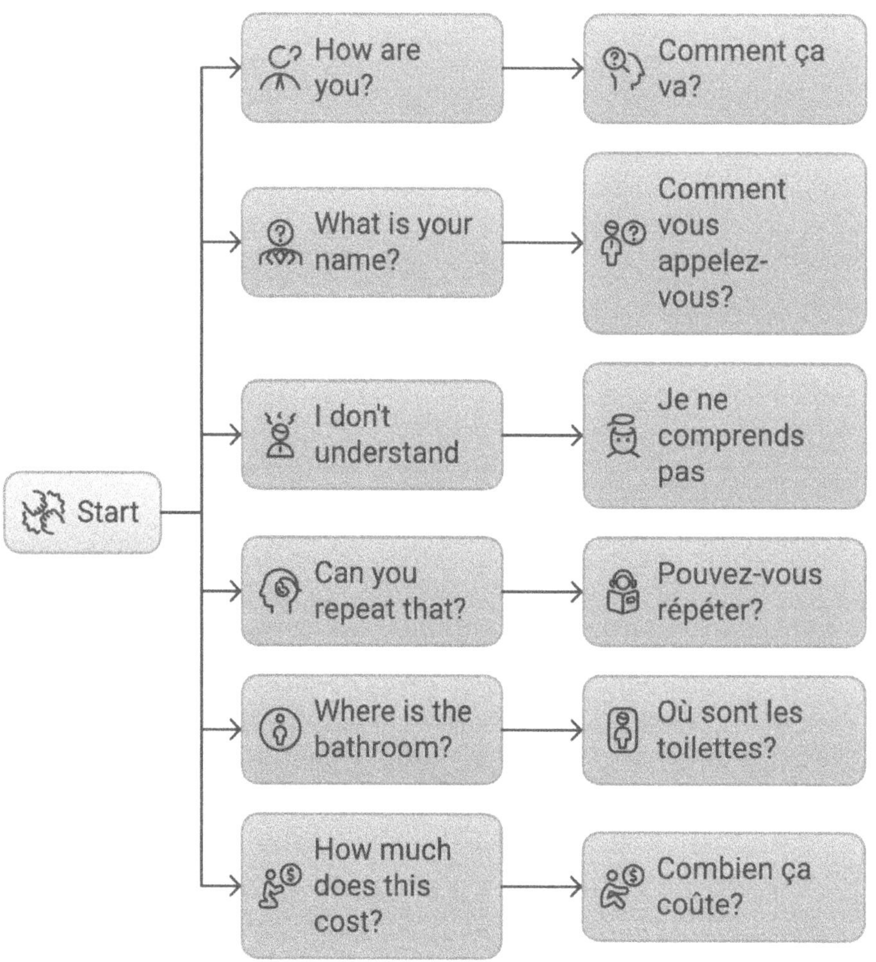

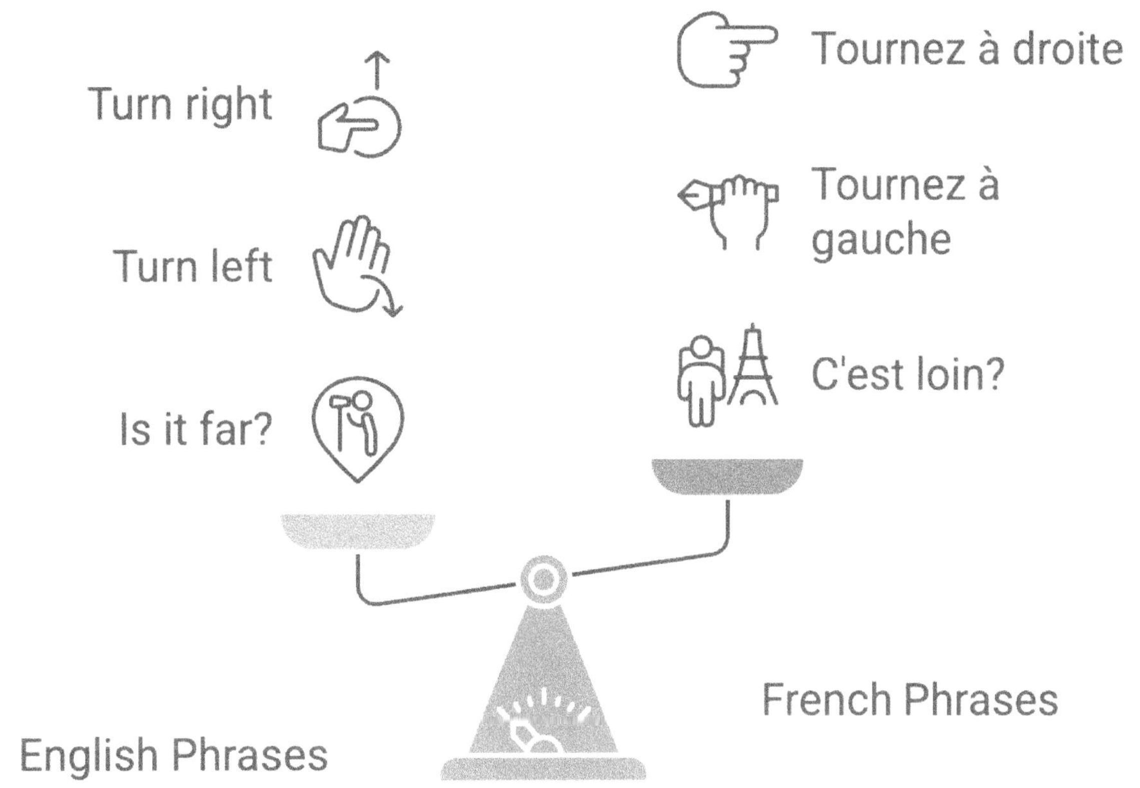

Navigate with ease in English or French.

Greetings in English and French

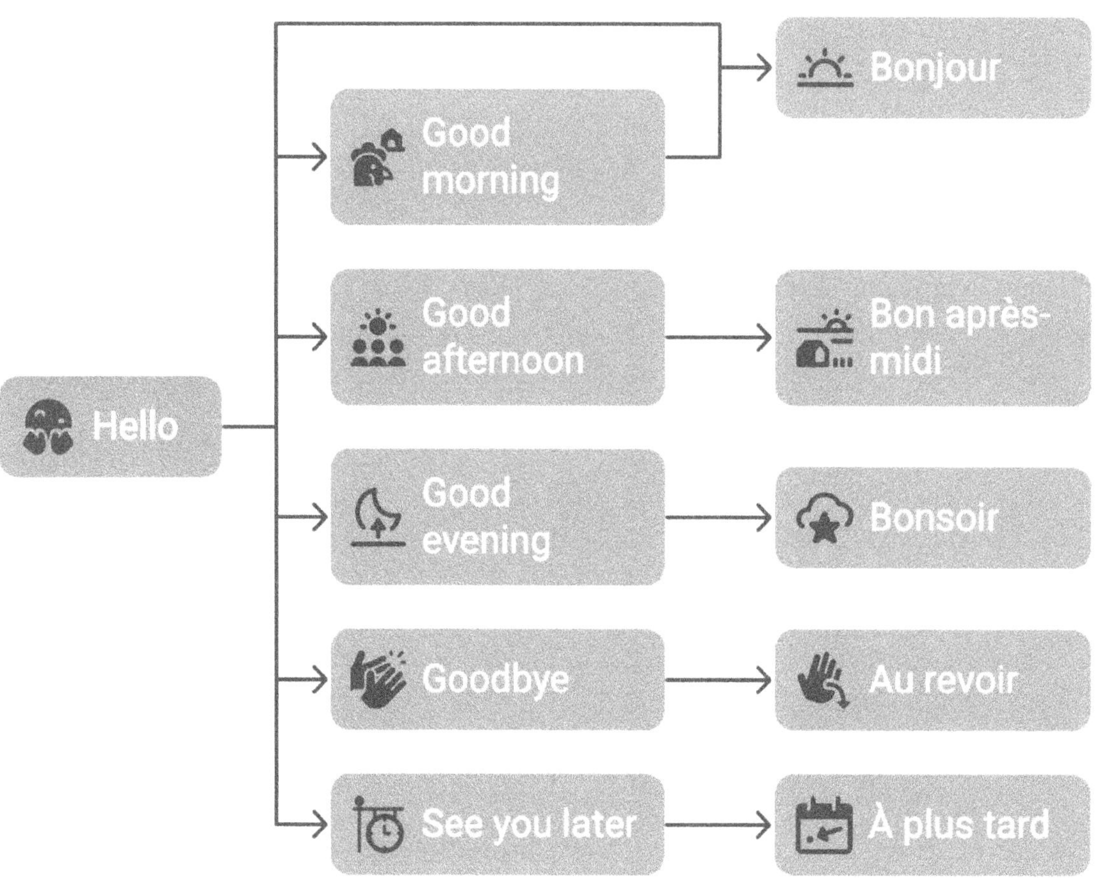

Greetings

English Greetings

Hello, A standard greeting is used at any time of the day.

Good morning: Typically used until noon.

Good afternoon: Used from noon until early evening.

Good evening: Used in the evening, usually after 5 or 6 PM.

Hi: A casual and informal greeting.

French Greetings

Bonjour: Equivalent to "Hello" or "Good morning," used until the evening.

Bonsoir: Used to say "Good evening," typically after 5 or 6 PM.

Salut: A casual greeting similar to "Hi" used among friends.

Introductions

English Introductions

My name is [Name]: A standard way to introduce oneself.

What is your name?: A polite inquiry to learn someone else's name.

Nice to meet you: A courteous expression is used after introductions.

French Introductions

Je m'appelle [Name]: The French equivalent of "My name is [Name]."

Comment vous appelez-vous?: A formal way to ask, "What is your name?"

Enchanté(e): This means "Nice to meet you." The extra "e" is added if the speaker is female.

Learning French is a journey that requires practice and patience. Keep practising these basic phrases daily, and soon, you'll be more comfortable with the language. Bonne chance! (Good luck!)

Multiple Choice Questions (MCQs)

What is the French equivalent of "Hello"?

a) Salut

b) Bonjour

c) Bonsoir

d) Bonne chance

Answer: b) Bonjour

When is "Good morning" typically used in English?

a) Anytime

b) Until noon

c) From noon to evening

d) After 6 PM

Answer: b) Until noon

Which French greeting is most similar to "Hi" in English?

a) Bonjour

b) Bonsoir

c) Salut

d) Enchanté

Answer: c) Salut

What is the English equivalent of "Bonsoir"?

a) Hello

b) Good evening

c) Good night

d) Goodbye

Answer: b) Good evening

How do you ask "What is your name?" in formal French?

a) Comment tu t'appelles?

b) Comment vous appelez-vous?

c) Comment allez-vous?

d) Qui es-tu?

Answer: b) Comment vous appelez-vous?

What is the casual way to greet a friend in French?

a) Bonsoir

b) Bonjour

c) Salut

d) Enchanté

Answer: c) Salut

What is the response to "Nice to meet you" in French?

a) Bonne chance

b) Salut

c) Enchanté(e)

d) Merci

Answer: c) Enchanté(e)

Which greeting would you use in English at 7 PM?

a) Good morning

b) Good afternoon

c) Good evening

d) Hello

Answer: c) Good evening

"Je m'appelle Sophie" means:

a) My name is Sophie

b) How are you, Sophie?

c) I am Sophie

d) See you later, Sophie

Answer: a) My name is Sophie

When do you typically use "Bonsoir" in French?

a) Morning

b) Noon

c) Evening

d) Anytime

Answer: c) Evening

What does "Bonne chance!" mean?

a) Good evening

b) Good night

c) Good luck

d) Goodbye

Answer: c) Good luck

Which phrase is used to meet someone in English politely?

a) Hello

b) Nice to meet you

c) How old are you?

d) Where do you live?

Answer: b) Nice to meet you

What does "Comment vous appelez-vous?" mean?

a) How are you?

b) What is your name?

c) Where are you from?

d) How old are you?

Answer: b) What is your name?

Which English greeting is the most formal?

a) Hi

b) Hey

c) Good morning

d) Yo

Answer: c) Good morning

What is the informal way to ask someone's name in French?

a) Comment vous appelez-vous?

b) Comment tu t'appelles?

c) Bonjour

d) Salut

Answer: b) Comment tu t'appelles?

Which greeting is not used in English?

a) Hello

b) Good evening

c) Bonjour

d) Hi

Answer: c) Bonjour

When do you use "Good afternoon" in English?

a) Before noon

b) From noon to early evening

c) After 8 PM

d) Anytime

Answer: b) From noon to early evening

Which French greeting is appropriate for a formal setting?

a) Salut

b) Bonjour

c) Yo

d) Hey

Answer: b) Bonjour

What does "Salut" mean in French?

a) Good night

b) Hello

c) Goodbye

d) Both b and c

Answer: d) Both b and c

Which greeting would you use when meeting a stranger at a formal event in French?

a) Salut

b) Bonsoir

c) Bonjour

d) Yo

Answer: c) Bonjour

What is the best way to introduce yourself in French?

a) Bonjour, je m'appelle [Name]

b) Salut, comment ça va?

c) Bonsoir, merci beaucoup

d) Comment vous appelez-vous?

Answer: a) Bonjour, je m'appelle [Name]

What does "Nice to meet you" translate to in French?

a) Enchanté(e)

b) Bonjour

c) Bonne chance

d) Merci

Answer: a) Enchanté(e)

Which phrase means "Good luck" in French?

a) Bonne nuit

b) Bonne chance

c) Bonsoir

d) Salut

Answer: b) Bonne chance

Which greeting is NOT time-specific?

a) Hello

b) Good morning

c) Good evening

d) Good afternoon

Answer: a) Hello

What is the most appropriate greeting for a business meeting in the morning?

a) Hey

b) Good morning

c) Salut

d) Hi

Answer: b) Good morning

CHAPTER FOUR

ASKING FOR DIRECTIONS

Common French Phrases for Asking Directions

Excusez-moi, pouvez-vous m'aider?

The French equivalent of "Excuse me, can you help me?" It is a polite way to ask for assistance.

Où est...?

This translates to "Where is...?" For example, "Où est la gare?" (Where is the train station?)

Comment puis-je aller à...?

This means, "How do I get to...?" For example, "Comment puis-je aller à l'aéroport?" (How do I get to the airport?)

C'est loin d'ici?

This translates to "Is it far from here?" It helps you gauge the distance to your destination.

Pouvez-vous me montrer sur la carte?

This means, "Can you show me on the map?" This is a helpful phrase when you need visual guidance.

Tournez à gauche/droite.

This means "Turn left/right." These are standard instructions you might receive.

French Vocabulary of Directions

Gauche: Left. Droite: Right. Tout droit: Straight. Près: Near. Loin: Far.

Mastering French Directions

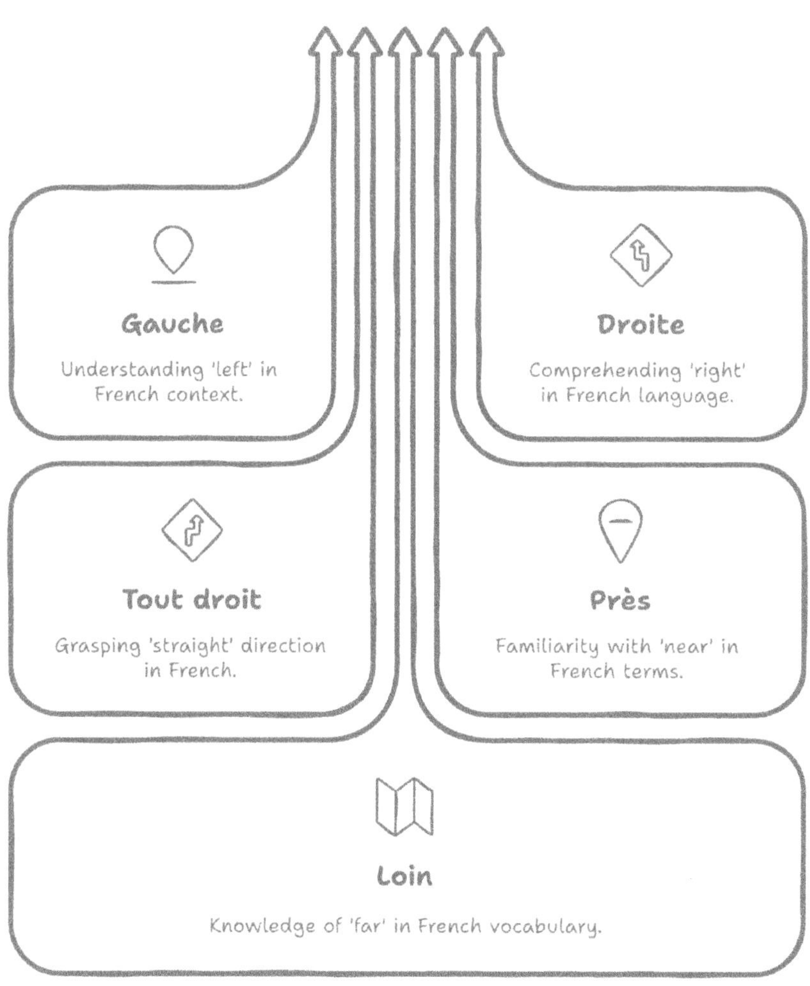

Multiple Choice Questions (MCQs)

1. What does "Excusez-moi, pouvez-vous m'aider?" mean in English?

a) Can you repeat that?

b) Excuse me, can you help me?

c) Where is the train station?

d) How do I get to the airport?

Answer: b) Excuse me, can you help me?

2. What is the French phrase for "Where is...?"

a) Comment puis-je aller à...?

b) Où est...?

c) Tournez à gauche.

d) C'est loin d'ici?

Answer: b) Où est...?

3. What would you say if you want to ask "How do I get to the airport?" in French?

a) Où est l'aéroport?

b) Comment puis-je aller à l'aéroport?

c) Tournez à droite.

d) C'est loin d'ici?

Answer: b) Comment puis-je aller à l'aéroport?

4. How do you ask if a place is far from your location?

a) Pouvez-vous me montrer sur la carte?

b) Où est la gare?

c) C'est loin d'ici?

d) Comment puis-je aller à l'aéroport?

Answer: c) C'est loin d'ici?

5. What should you say if you want someone to show you a place on a map?

a) Tournez à droite.

b) Pouvez-vous me montrer sur la carte?

c) Où est...?

d) C'est loin d'ici?

Answer: b) Pouvez-vous me montrer sur la carte?

6. What is the French word for "left"?

a) Droite

b) Gauche

c) Tout droit

d) Près

Answer: b) Gauche

7. What does "Tournez à droite" mean?

a) Go straight

b) Turn right

c) Turn left

d) Near

Answer: b) Turn right

8. To tell someone to "Go straight," which French phrase should you use?

a) Tournez à gauche

b) Tout droit

c) Près

d) Loin

Answer: b) Tout droit

9. What is the opposite of "Près" (Near) in French?

a) Loin

b) Gauche

c) Droite

d) Tout droit

Answer: a) Loin

10. What does "Où est la gare?" mean in English?

a) Where is the train station?

b) Where is the airport?

c) Where is the bus stop?

d) Where is the hotel?

Answer: a) Where is the train station?

11. If someone tells you "Tournez à gauche," what should you do?

a) Turn right

b) Turn left

c) Go straight

d) Stop

Answer: b) Turn left

12. What does "Pouvez-vous me montrer sur la carte?" mean?

a) Can you help me?

b) Can you show me on the map?

c) Where is the nearest restaurant?

d) Is it far from here?

Answer: b) Can you show me on the map?

13. If someone says "C'est loin d'ici," what does that mean?

a) It is near here.

b) It is far from here.

c) Turn left.

d) Turn right.

Answer: b) It is far from here.

14. How do you ask where the airport is?

a) Où est l'aéroport?

b) Où est la gare?

c) Comment puis-je aller à l'hôtel?

d) Pouvez-vous me montrer sur la carte?

Answer: a) Où est l'aéroport?

15. What does "Droite" mean in English?

a) Left

b) Right

c) Straight

d) Far

Answer: b) Right

16. What would you say if you want to say "Turn left" in French?

a) Tournez à droite

b) Tournez à gauche

c) Tout droit

d) C'est loin d'ici

Answer: b) Tournez à gauche

17. If someone says "Près," what does that mean?

a) Near

b) Far

c) Right

d) Left

Answer: a) Near

18. What does "Comment puis-je aller à..." help you do?

a) Ask where something is

b) Ask how to get somewhere

c) Ask if a place is near

d) Ask for a map

Answer: b) Ask how to get somewhere

19. How do you ask French, "Where is the hotel?"?

a) Où est l'hôtel?

b) Comment puis-je aller à l'hôtel?

c) Pouvez-vous me montrer sur la carte?

d) C'est loin d'ici?

Answer: a) Où est l'hôtel?

20. If someone says "Tout droit," what should you do?

a) Turn left

b) Turn right

c) Go straight

d) Stop

Answer: c) Go straight

CHAPTER FIVE

AT A RESTAURANT

Common Phrases

Greeting the Staff

English: Hello! / Good evening!

French: Bonjour ! / Bonsoir !

Asking for a Table

English: Do you have a table for two?

French: Avez-vous une table pour deux ?

Looking at the Menu

English: Can I see the menu, please?

French: Puis-je voir le menu, s'il vous plaît ?

Ordering Food

English: I would like to order...

French: Je voudrais commander...

Asking About the Specials

English: What are the specials today?

French: Quels sont les plats du jour ?

Making a Special Request

English: Can I have this without nuts?

French: Puis-je avoir cela sans noix ?

Asking for Recommendations

English: What do you recommend?

French: Que recommandez-vous ?

Ordering Drinks

English: I would like a glass of red wine.

French: Je voudrais un verre de vin rouge.

Asking for the Bill

English: Can I have the bill, please?

French: Puis-je avoir l'addition, s'il vous plaît ?

Complimenting the Meal

English: The food was delicious!

French: La nourriture était délicieuse !

Saying Goodbye

English: Thank you! Have a great day!

French: Merci ! Passez une bonne journée !

<u>Vocabulary</u>

Food Items

English: Chicken / Fish / Salad / Dessert

French: Poulet / Poisson / Salade / Dessert

Drinks

English: Water / Beer / Wine / Juice

French: Eau / Bière / Vin / Jus

Common Adjectives

English: Spicy / Sweet / Salty / Sour

French: Épicé / Sucré / Salé / Acide

Multiple Choice Questions (MCQs)

1. When greeting the staff, what is the French equivalent of "Hello!"?
a) Bonsoir
b) Bonjour
c) Merci
d) Au revoir
Answer: b) Bonjour

2. How do you ask for a table for two in French?
a) Puis-je voir le menu, s'il vous plaît ?
b) Avez-vous une table pour deux ?
c) Que recommandez-vous ?
d) Puis-je avoir l'addition, s'il vous plaît ?
Answer: b) Avez-vous une table pour deux ?

3. What does "Puis-je voir le menu, s'il vous plaît ?" mean?
a) Can I see the menu, please?
b) What do you recommend?
c) Can I have the bill, please?
d) Do you have a table for two?
Answer: a) Can I see the menu, please?

4. What is the correct translation for "What are the specials today?"
a) Quels sont les plats du jour ?
b) Que recommandez-vous ?
c) La nourriture était délicieuse !
d) Puis-je avoir l'addition, s'il vous plaît ?
Answer: a) Quels sont les plats du jour ?

5. How do you ask "Can I have this without nuts?" in French?
a) Puis-je voir le menu, s'il vous plaît ?
b) Puis-je avoir cela sans noix ?

c) Puis-je avoir l'addition, s'il vous plaît ?

d) Que recommandez-vous ?

Answer: b) Puis-je avoir cela sans noix ?

6. What does "Que recommandez-vous ?" mean?

a) What do you recommend?

b) What are the specials today?

c) Can I have this without nuts?

d) Can I see the menu, please?

Answer: a) What do you recommend?

7. If you want to order a drink and say, "I would like a glass of red wine," how do you say it in French?

a) Je voudrais un verre de vin rouge.

b) Puis-je voir le menu, s'il vous plaît ?

c) Avez-vous une table pour deux ?

d) Puis-je avoir l'addition, s'il vous plaît ?

Answer: a) Je voudrais un verre de vin rouge.

8. How do you politely ask for the bill in French?

a) Puis-je avoir cela sans noix ?

b) Puis-je avoir l'addition, s'il vous plaît ?

c) Que recommandez-vous ?

d) La nourriture était délicieuse !

Answer: b) Puis-je avoir l'addition, s'il vous plaît ?

9. What does "La nourriture était délicieuse !" mean?

a) The food was delicious!

b) Can I have the bill, please?

c) What do you recommend?

d) The food was too salty.

Answer: a) The food was delicious!

10. What is the French word for "Chicken"?

a) Poisson

b) Poulet

c) Salade

d) Dessert

Answer: b) Poulet

11. How do you say "Wine" in French?

a) Eau

b) Bière

c) Vin

d) Jus

Answer: c) Vin

12. What is the French translation for "Juice"?

a) Bière

b) Jus

c) Eau

d) Poisson

Answer: b) Jus

13. How do you say "Spicy" in French?

a) Épicé

b) Sucré

c) Salé

d) Acide

Answer: a) Épicé

14. If a dish is "Sucré," what does it mean in English?

a) Sour

b) Spicy

c) Sweet

d) Salty

Answer: c) Sweet

15. What is the French word for "Salty"?

a) Épicé

b) Sucré

c) Salé

d) Acide

Answer: c) Salé

16. If something is "Acide" in French, how would you describe it in English?

a) Spicy

b) Sour

c) Sweet

d) Salty

Answer: b) Sour

17. What is the correct French translation for "Good evening!"?

a) Bonjour !

b) Bonsoir !

c) Merci !

d) La nourriture était délicieuse !

Answer: b) Bonsoir !

18. What would you say if you want to thank the restaurant staff and say "Thank you! Have a great day!" in French?

a) Merci ! Passez une bonne journée !

b) Bonsoir ! Passez une bonne journée !

c) Que recommandez-vous ?

d) Puis-je voir le menu, s'il vous plaît ?

Answer: a) Merci ! Passez une bonne journée !

19. What is the French translation for "Fish"?

a) Poulet

b) Poisson

c) Salade

d) Dessert

Answer: b) Poisson

20. How do you say "I would like to order..." in French?

a) Je voudrais commander...

b) La nourriture était délicieuse !

c) Avez-vous une table pour deux ?

d) Puis-je avoir cela sans noix ?

Answer: a) Je voudrais commander...

Common Conversations in a School Among Kids

1. Greeting Each Other

English:

A: "Hi! How are you?"

B: "I'm good, thanks! And you?"

French:

A: "Salut ! Comment ça va ?"

B: "Ça va bien, merci ! Et toi ?"

2. Asking About Homework

English:

A: "Did you finish the math homework?"

B: "Not yet, it's really hard!"

French:

A: "Tu as fini les devoirs de maths ?"

B: "Pas encore, c'est vraiment difficile !"

3. Talking About Lunch

English:

A: "What did you bring for lunch?"

B: "I have a sandwich and some fruit."

French:

A: "Qu'est-ce que tu as apporté pour le déjeuner ?"

B: "J'ai un sandwich et des fruits."

4. Discussing Favorite Subjects

English:

A: "What's your favorite subject?"

B: "I love science! What about you?"

French:

A: "Quelle est ta matière préférée ?"

B: "J'adore les sciences ! Et toi ?"

5. Making Plans for the Weekend

English:

A: "Do you want to hang out this weekend?"

B: "Sure! What do you want to do?"

French:

A: "Tu veux sortir ce week-end ?"

B: "Bien sûr ! Que veux-tu faire ?"

6. Complimenting Each Other

English:

A: "I like your backpack!"

B: "Thanks! I got it for my birthday."

French:

A: "J'aime ton sac à dos !"

B: "Merci ! Je l'ai eu pour mon anniversaire."

7. Asking for Help

English:

A: "Can you help me with this problem?"

B: "Of course! Let's work on it together."

French:

A: "Peux-tu m'aider avec ce problème ?"

B: "Bien sûr ! Travaillons dessus ensemble."

8. Talking About Sports

English:

A: "Do you play soccer?"

B: "Yes, I play on the school team!"

French:

A: "Tu joues au foot ?"

B: "Oui, je joue dans l'équipe de l'école !"

9. Sharing News

English:

A: "Did you hear about the school trip?"

B: "Yes! I'm so excited!"

French:

A: "As-tu entendu parler de la sortie scolaire ?"

B: "Oui ! Je suis tellement excité !"

10. Saying Goodbye

English:

A: "See you tomorrow!"

B: "Bye! Have a great day!"

French:

A: "À demain !"

B: "Au revoir ! Passe une bonne journée !"

At the Shopping Mall

Asking for Directions

English:

A: Excuse me, can you tell me where the nearest restroom is?

B: Sure! It's down the hall, to the left.

French:

A: Excusez-moi, pouvez-vous me dire où se trouve les toilettes les plus proches ?

B: Bien sûr ! C'est au bout du couloir, à gauche.

Shopping for Clothes

English:

A: Do you have this shirt in a larger size?

B: Let me check for you. What size do you need?

French:

A: Avez-vous cette chemise dans une taille plus grande ?

B: Laissez-moi vérifier pour vous. Quelle taille vous faut-il ?

Asking About Prices

English:

A: How much is this jacket?

B: It's $50, but there's a sale today!

French:

A: Combien coûte cette veste ?

B: C'est 50 dollars, mais il y a une promotion aujourd'hui !

In a Public Place

Asking for Help

English:

A: Can you help me find this address?

B: Of course! Where is it located?

French:

A: Pouvez-vous m'aider à trouver cette adresse ?

B: Bien sûr ! Où se trouve t-elle ?

Ordering Food

English:

A: I would like a coffee and a croissant, please.

B: That will be $5. Would you like anything else?

French:

A: Je voudrais un café et un croissant, s'il vous plaît.

B: Cela fera 5 dollars. Voulez-vous autre chose ?

Asking for Recommendations

English:

A: What restaurant do you recommend around here?

B: There's a great Italian place just down the street!

French:

A: Quel restaurant recommandez-vous dans le coin ?

B: Il y a un excellent restaurant italien juste au bout de la rue !

Multiple-Choice Questions (MCQs)

1. How do you say "Hi! How are you?" in French?
a) Salut ! Comment ça va ?
b) Bonjour ! Comment vous appelez-vous ?
c) Salut ! Où est la gare ?
d) Bonjour ! Où est le restaurant ?
Answer: a) Salut ! Comment ça va ?

2. What is the correct response in French to "Ça va bien, merci ! Et toi ?"
a) Salut !
b) Au revoir !
c) Moi aussi, merci !
d) Comment vous appelez-vous ?
Answer: c) Moi aussi, merci !

3. What is the French translation of "Did you finish the math homework?"
a) As-tu entendu parler de la sortie scolaire ?
b) Tu as fini les devoirs de maths ?
c) Peux-tu m'aider avec ce problème ?
d) Tu joues au foot ?
Answer: b) Tu as fini les devoirs de maths ?

4. What does "Pas encore, c'est vraiment difficile !" mean?
a) Not yet, it's really hard!

b) Yes, I finished it!

c) I don't have any homework.

d) The test was easy!

Answer: a) Not yet, it's really hard!

    5. How do you ask "What did you bring for lunch?" in French?

a) Qu'est-ce que tu as apporté pour le déjeuner ?

b) Quelle est ta matière préférée ?

c) Que recommandez-vous ?

d) Avez-vous cette chemise dans une taille plus grande ?

Answer: a) Qu'est-ce que tu as apporté pour le déjeuner ?

    6. How do you say "I have a sandwich and some fruit" in French?

a) J'adore les sciences !

b) J'ai un sandwich et des fruits.

c) J'ai une salade et un dessert.

d) C'est 50 dollars, mais il y a une promotion aujourd'hui !

Answer: b) J'ai un sandwich et des fruits.

    7. What is the French equivalent of "What's your favorite subject?"

a) Tu veux sortir ce week-end ?

b) Peux-tu m'aider avec ce problème ?

c) Quelle est ta matière préférée ?

d) Avez-vous une table pour deux ?

Answer: c) Quelle est ta matière préférée ?

    8. How do you say "I love science! What about you?" in French?

a) J'adore les sciences ! Et toi ?

b) Je voudrais un verre de vin rouge.

c) Oui, je joue dans l'équipe de l'école !

d) Puis-je voir le menu, s'il vous plaît ?

Answer: a) J'adore les sciences ! Et toi ?

    9. What does "Tu veux sortir ce week-end ?" mean?

a) Do you want to go out this weekend?

b) What did you bring for lunch?

c) What is your favorite subject?

d) Can you help me with this problem?

Answer: a) Do you want to go out this weekend?

10. How do you respond to "Bien sûr ! Que veux-tu faire ?" in English?

a) Sure! What do you want to do?

b) No, I have plans.

c) Yes, I love football!

d) What is your name?

Answer: a) Sure! What do you want to do?

11. What does "Excusez-moi, pouvez-vous me dire où se trouve les toilettes les plus proches ?" mean?

a) Excuse me, can you tell me where the nearest restroom is?

b) Can you help me find this address?

c) Where is the restaurant?

d) What do you recommend?

Answer: a) Excuse me, can you tell me where the nearest restroom is?

12. How do you say "It's down the hall, to the left" in French?

a) C'est au bout du couloir, à gauche.

b) Il y a un excellent restaurant italien juste au bout de la rue !

c) Puis-je avoir l'addition, s'il vous plaît ?

d) C'est vraiment difficile !

Answer: a) C'est au bout du couloir, à gauche.

13. How do you ask "Do you have this shirt in a larger size?" in French?

a) Avez-vous cette chemise dans une taille plus grande ?

b) Puis-je avoir l'addition, s'il vous plaît ?

c) Que recommandez-vous ?

d) Peux-tu m'aider avec ce problème ?

Answer: a) Avez-vous cette chemise dans une taille plus grande ?

14. What does "Quelle taille vous faut-il ?" mean?

a) What size do you need?

b) Where is the restroom?

c) Do you play soccer?

d) How much does this jacket cost?

Answer: a) What size do you need?

15. What does "Je voudrais un café et un croissant, s'il vous plaît." mean?

a) I would like a coffee and a croissant, please.

b) Do you have a table for two?

c) I love science!

d) What is your favorite restaurant?

Answer: a) I would like a coffee and a croissant, please.

16. How do you say "That will be $5. Would you like anything else?" in French?

a) Cela fera 5 dollars. Voulez-vous autre chose ?

b) C'cst 50 dollars, mais il y a unc promotion aujourd'hui !

c) Peux-tu m'aider avec ce problème ?

d) Avez-vous une table pour deux ?

Answer: a) Cela fera 5 dollars. Voulez-vous autre chose ?

17. How do you say "What restaurant do you recommend around here?" in French?

a) Quel restaurant recommandez-vous dans le coin ?

b) Avez-vous une table pour deux ?

c) Peux-tu m'aider avec ce problème ?

d) Quelle est ta matière préférée ?

Answer: a) Quel restaurant recommandez-vous dans le coin ?

18. How do you respond to "Il y a un excellent restaurant italien juste au bout de la rue !" in English?

a) There's a great Italian place just down the street!

b) I would like a coffee, please.

c) Do you play soccer?

d) The jacket is $50.

Answer: a) There's a great Italian place just down the street!

100 Most Common Vocabulary

ENGLISH- FRENCH

the - le, la, les

be - être

to - à

of - de

and - et

a - un, une

in - dans

that - que

have - avoir

I - je

it - il, elle

for - pour

not - pas

on - sur

with - avec

he - il

as - comme

you - tu, vous

do - faire

at - à

this - ce, cette

but - mais

his - son

by - par

from - de

they - ils, elles

we - nous

say - dire

her - son, sa

she - elle

or - ou

an - un, une

will - volonté, futur

my - mon, ma

one - un, une

all - tout

would - serait

there - là

their - leur

what - quoi

so - donc

up - en haut

out - dehors

if - si

about - environ

who - qui

get - obtenir

which - lequel

go - aller

me - moi

when - quand

make - faire

can - pouvoir

like - comme, aimer

time - temps

no - non

just - juste

him - lui

know - savoir

take - prendre

people - gens

into - dans

year - année

your - ton, votre

good - bon

some - quelques

could - pourrait

them - eux, elles

see - voir

other - autre

than - que

then - alors

now - maintenant

look - regarder

only - seulement

come - venir

its - son, sa

over - sur

think - penser

also - aussi

back - dos, retour

after - après

use - utiliser

two - deux

how - comment

our - notre

work - travail

first - premier

well - bien

way - manière

even - même

new - nouveau

want - vouloir

because - parce que

any - aucun

these - ces

give - donner

day - jour

most - plus

us - nous

Multiple-Choice Questions (MCQs)

1. What is the French word for "the"?

a) un

b) être

c) le, la, les

d) sur

Answer: c) le, la, les

2. How do you say "I" in French?

a) tu

b) vous

c) il

d) je

Answer: d) je

3. What is the French equivalent of "and"?

a) ou

b) et

c) avec

d) comme

Answer: b) et

4. Which French word means "for"?

a) avec

b) pour

c) sur

d) dans

Answer: b) pour

5. What is the French translation of "they"?

a) ils, elles

b) nous

c) vous

d) son

Answer: a) ils, elles

6. How do you say "with" in French?

a) sur

b) par

c) avec

d) comme

Answer: c) avec

7. Which of the following means "no" in French?

a) si

b) non

c) oui

d) alors

Answer: b) non

8. What is the French word for "time"?

a) année

b) jour

c) temps

d) moment

Answer: c) temps

9. How do you say "look" in French?

a) penser

b) voir

c) regarder

d) savoir

Answer: c) regarder

10. What is the French translation of "first"?

a) premier

b) deuxième

c) autre

d) tout

Answer: a) premier

11. Which of these words means "on" in French?

a) à

b) sur

c) dans

d) de

Answer: b) sur

12. What is the French word for "if"?

a) si

b) alors

c) que

d) où

Answer: a) si

13. How do you say "because" in French?

a) ou

b) parce que

c) alors

d) donc

Answer: b) parce que

14. What is the French translation of "when"?

a) comment

b) quand

c) où

d) qui

Answer: b) quand

15. What does "donc" mean in English?

a) so

b) from

c) over

d) which

Answer: a) so

16. How do you say "take" in French?

a) voir

b) prendre

c) dire

d) venir

Answer: b) prendre

17. Which word means "make" in French?

a) pouvoir

b) faire

c) dire

d) être

Answer: b) faire

18. What is the French translation of "see"?

a) savoir

b) prendre

c) voir

d) regarder

Answer: c) voir

19. Which of the following means "give" in French?

a) obtenir

b) donner

c) vouloir

d) savoir

Answer: b) donner

20. What does "travailler" mean in English?

a) time

b) work

c) say

d) look

Answer: b) work

CHAPTER EIGHT

100 COMMONLY USED SENTENCES IN FRENCH

Greetings and Introductions

Bonjour - Hello / Good morning.

Bonsoir - Good evening.

Salut - Hi / Bye (informal).

Comment ça va ? - How are you?

Ça va bien, merci. - I'm fine, thank you.

Et toi ? - And you? (informal)

Enchanté(e). - Nice to meet you.

Comment tu t'appelles ? - What's your name?

Je m'appelle... - My name is...

D'où viens-tu ? - Where are you from?

Basic Questions

Qu'est-ce que c'est ? - What is this?

Où est... ? - Where is...?

Qui est-ce ? - Who is this?

Quand est-ce que... ? - When is...?

Pourquoi ? - Why?

Comment ? - How?

Combien ça coûte ? - How much does it cost?

Est-ce que tu parles anglais ? - Do you speak English?

Pouvez-vous m'aider ? - Can you help me?

Qu'est-ce que tu fais ? - What are you doing?

Everyday Expressions

S'il vous plaît. - Please.

Merci. - Thank you.

De rien. - You're welcome.

Excusez-moi. - Excuse me.

Je suis désolé(e). - I'm sorry.

Pas de problème. - No problem.

D'accord. - Okay.

Bien sûr. - Of course.

Je ne sais pas. - I don't know.

Je ne comprends pas. - I don't understand.

Directions and Travel

Où est la gare ? - Where is the train station?

Où sont les toilettes ? - Where is the bathroom?

Je suis perdu(e). - I'm lost.

À droite. - To the right.

À gauche. - To the left.

Tout droit. - Straight ahead.

C'est loin ? - Is it far?

Je cherche... - I'm looking for...

Un billet pour Paris, s'il vous plaît. - A ticket to Paris, please.

Quel est le prochain arrêt ? - What is the next stop?

Shopping and Dining

Je voudrais... - I would like...

L'addition, s'il vous plaît. - The bill, please.

C'est combien ? - How much is it?

Avez-vous... ? - Do you have...?

Je vais prendre ça. - I'll take this.

C'est trop cher. - It's too expensive.

Je voudrais réserver une table. - I'd like to book a table.

Qu'est-ce que vous recommandez ? - What do you recommend?

Je suis végétarien(ne). - I'm vegetarian.

Une carafe d'eau, s'il vous plaît. - A carafe of water, please.

Time and Dates

Quelle heure est-il ? - What time is it?

Il est midi. - It's noon.

Il est minuit. - It's midnight.

Aujourd'hui. - Today.

Demain. - Tomorrow.

Hier. - Yesterday.

Le matin. - In the morning.

L'après-midi. - In the afternoon.

Le soir. - In the evening.

Quel jour sommes-nous ? - What day is it?

Feelings and Opinions

Je suis fatigué(e). - I'm tired.

Je suis content(e). - I'm happy.

Je suis triste. - I'm sad.

J'ai faim. - I'm hungry.

J'ai soif. - I'm thirsty.

J'ai chaud. - I'm hot.

J'ai froid. - I'm cold.

C'est bon. - It's good.

C'est mauvais. - It's bad.

J'aime ça. - I like it.

At Home

Où est la clé ? - Where is the key?

Je rentre à la maison. - I'm going home.

Je vais dormir. - I'm going to sleep.

Qu'est-ce qu'on mange ? - What are we eating?

Fais attention ! - Be careful!

Nettoyez votre chambre. - Clean your room.

Je vais prendre une douche. - I'm going to take a shower.

Allume la lumière. - Turn on the light.

Éteins la télé. - Turn off the TV.

Je vais faire les courses. - I'm going grocery shopping.

Work and School

Je travaille. - I'm working.

Je suis en retard. - I'm late.

J'ai un rendez-vous. - I have an appointment.

Quel est ton métier ? - What is your job?

Je suis étudiant(e). - I'm a student.

J'ai un examen demain. - I have an exam tomorrow.

C'est difficile. - It's difficult.

C'est facile. - It's easy.

Je dois étudier. - I have to study.

Je vais au bureau. - I'm going to the office.

Health and Emergencies

J'ai mal à la tête. - I have a headache.

J'ai besoin d'un médecin. - I need a doctor.

Appelez une ambulance ! - Call an ambulance!

Où est l'hôpital ? - Where is the hospital?

Je suis malade. - I'm sick.

Aidez-moi ! - Help me!

Je suis allergique à... - I'm allergic to...

Où est la pharmacie ? - Where is the pharmacy?

J'ai perdu mon passeport. - I lost my passport.

Au secours ! - Help!

Multiple-Choice Questions (MCQs)

1. How do you say "Hello" in French?

a) Salut

b) Bonjour

c) Bonsoir

d) Merci

Answer: b) Bonjour

2. What does "Enchanté(e)" mean?

a) How are you?

b) Nice to meet you

c) Where are you from?

d) See you later

Answer: b) Nice to meet you

3. Which phrase means "What's your name?" in French?

a) Comment ça va ?

b) Comment tu t'appelles ?

c) Je m'appelle...

d) Qui est-ce ?

Answer: b) Comment tu t'appelles ?

4. How do you say "Where are you from?" in French?

a) D'où viens-tu ?

b) Où est... ?

c) Qu'est-ce que tu fais ?

d) Quelle heure est-il ?

Answer: a) D'où viens-tu ?

5. "Où est..." means:

a) How much is it?

b) Where is...?

c) When is it?

d) Who is this?

Answer: b) Where is...?

6. What is the French translation of "How much does it cost?"

a) Combien ça coûte ?

b) Comment ça va ?

c) Où est... ?

d) Pourquoi ?

Answer: a) Combien ça coûte ?

7. Which phrase means "Can you help me?"

a) Pouvez-vous m'aider ?

b) Qu'est-ce que c'est ?

c) Je suis fatigué(e).

d) Où sont les toilettes ?

Answer: a) Pouvez-vous m'aider ?

8. How do you ask "What are you doing?" in French?

a) Qu'est-ce que tu fais ?

b) Qui est-ce ?

c) Quel est le prochain arrêt ?

d) Je vais dormir.

Answer: a) Qu'est-ce que tu fais ?

9. How do you say "Thank you" in French?

a) De rien

b) Merci

c) Excusez-moi

d) D'accord

Answer: b) Merci

10. What does "Je suis désolé(e)" mean?

a) I don't understand

b) I'm sorry

c) You're welcome

d) No problem

Answer: b) I'm sorry

11. Which phrase means "Excuse me"?

a) Excusez-moi

b) Pas de problème

c) S'il vous plaît

d) Je ne sais pas

Answer: a) Excusez-moi

12. How do you say "Where is the bathroom?" in French?

a) Où est la gare ?

b) Où sont les toilettes ?

c) Je cherche...

d) C'est loin ?

Answer: b) Où sont les toilettes ?

13. Which phrase means "I'm lost"?

a) À gauche

b) Je suis perdu(e)

c) C'est loin ?

d) Tout droit

Answer: b) Je suis perdu(e)

14. "À gauche" means:

a) To the right

b) To the left

c) Straight ahead

d) It's far

Answer: b) To the left

15. What does "Je voudrais..." mean?

a) I would like...

b) I have...

c) How much is it?

d) I'm vegetarian

Answer: a) I would like...

16. How do you say "The bill, please" in French?

a) Une carafe d'eau, s'il vous plaît

b) L'addition, s'il vous plaît

c) Avez-vous... ?

d) Je vais prendre ça

Answer: b) L'addition, s'il vous plaît

17. "C'est trop cher" means:

a) It's very good

b) It's too expensive

c) I like it

d) It's delicious

Answer: b) It's too expensive

18. How do you say "What time is it?" in French?

a) Quelle heure est-il ?

b) Aujourd'hui

c) Quel jour sommes-nous ?

d) Il est minuit

Answer: a) Quelle heure est-il ?

19. "Hier" means:

a) Today

b) Tomorrow

c) Yesterday

d) Noon

Answer: c) Yesterday

20. How do you say "In the morning" in French?

a) Le matin

b) L'après-midi

c) Le soir

d) Minuit

Answer: a) Le matin

21. How do you say "I'm tired" in French?

a) J'ai soif

b) Je suis fatigué(e)

c) J'ai faim

d) Je suis content(e)

Answer: b) Je suis fatigué(e)

22. What does "J'ai froid" mean?

a) I'm hot

b) I'm cold

c) I'm hungry

d) I'm thirsty

Answer: b) I'm cold

23. Which of these phrases means "I have a headache"?

a) J'ai mal à la tête

b) Je suis malade

c) Appelez une ambulance !

d) Aidez-moi !

Answer: a) J'ai mal à la tête

24. How do you say "Call an ambulance!" in French?

a) Où est la pharmacie ?

b) Appelez une ambulance !

c) J'ai perdu mon passeport.

d) Je suis allergique à...

Answer: b) Appelez une ambulance !

25. "Où est l'hôpital ?" means:

a) Where is the pharmacy?

b) Where is the hospital?

c) Where is the bank?

d) Where is the train station?

Answer: b) Where is the hospital?

Scan Here
FOR QUALITY BOOKS
For Heads of Schools, Educators,
Parents & Students